Foundational Islamic Principles

Translated from

al-Muḥalla bil'Athār

المحلى بالآثار

by Ibn Ḥazm

http://www.renascencefoundation.com

ISBN: 1974097715
ISBN-13:9781974097715

Acknowledgements

Translation is never always an exact science, particularly when trying to render difficult legal texts from Arabic to English. Special thanks are therefore due to Professor Muhammad ibn Abdullah al-Mas'ari for his invaluable input and comment, as well as Shaykh Muhammad Abdul Basit Awan for the work completed in relation to chapter four. We are further indebted to Imran Choudhury for his diligent review of the manuscript and Nazim Uddin for the cover design and his expert technical support throughout. Lastly, special thanks are due to K. M. Hasan, for leading the project to translate this text.

Contents

Foreword i

1. The *Deen* of Islam is only to be taken from the Qur'ān or from the *Sunnah* 1

2. The *ḥadith mawquf* and *mursal* do not establish proof by themselves 3

3. The Qur'ān abrogates the Qur'ān and the *Sunnah* abrogates the *Sunnah* 8

4. Abrogation and specification in the Qur'ān & the *Sunnah* 10

5. Consensus is that which we are certain all the Companions of the Messenger of Allah knew 14

6. What is not consensus 16

7. It is not permissible that all people of a given generation can agree upon a mistake 17

8. Disagreements of the people or the dissent of one in relation to an issue 20

9. Analogy 22

10. Actions of the Prophet are not obligated except where accompanied with a clear statement of command 39

11. *Sharī'ah* of the previous Prophets 40

12. It is not permissible for anyone to imitate another, whether alive or dead 42

13. Questions from laymen to the people of Deen 47

14. No ruling applies for mistakes or forgetfulness 51

15. Every obligation Allah has obliged all of mankind to do........ 52

16. It is not permissible to perform acts outside of the delineated time parameters... 54

17. The jurist has a higher standing before Allah than the follower 57

18. Determining the one true viewpoint from among an array 59

Foreword

Ali ibn Aḥmad ibn Sa'eed ibn Ḥazm, Abu Muḥammad, that is Ibn Ḥazm, was born in Cordoba, Spain. His own lifespan (born 994 CE, died 1064 CE) covered a period of Islamic rule in Spain often characterised by political turbulence, but also regarded as being a golden age of Islamic civilization in Europe. A true polymath, the breadth of Ibn Ḥazm's works and overall contribution to knowledge is quite exceptional: not only spanning the full range of the Islamic sciences, but also including philosophy, ethics, literature, poetry and being credited with pioneering what has become the study of comparative religion.[1] Ibn Ḥazm's contribution to the rich tapestry of Islamic thought ranks no less to that of other famous polymaths like al-Ghazāli and Ibn Taymiyyah.

---

[1] Muslim scholars and biographers have alluded to Ibn Ḥazm being credited with works numbering over four-hundred volumes. Jose Vilchez has listed over 140 titles of known works. See: 'Inventory of Ibn Ḥazm's works,' by Jose Miguel Puerta Vilchez, in *Ibn Ḥazm of Cordoba: The Life and Works of a Controversial Thinker* (Boston: Brill), (ed) Camilla Adang, Maribel Fierro and Sabine Schmidtke, 2013, pp. 683/760

Yet the study of his works has not achieved the same precedence.[2] While often described as a being a radical and a free-thinker, Ibn Ḥazm's works have all too often been ignored or completely overlooked, not least in part because of the scathing criticisms he levelled against mainstream Islamic schools of thought.

For those actively looking to reinvigorate Islamic discourse, the works of Ibn Ḥazm are though quite invaluable. As has been noted by many commentators,[3] Ibn Ḥazm's works cannot be characterised as representing a *madhab* (legal school of thought) per se. Rather, the principles and approach that he sought to outline represent more of a *legal method*; one that is strictly based upon the texts of revelation: the Qur'ān and the Prophetic *Sunnah*. That method, outlined in voluminous works of *fiqh* (jurisprudence) and *Uṣul* shouldn't however be seen as an end product, like those of the current rigid schools, but rather a starting point.

For the first time in English, a complete translation of '*Masā'il min al-Uṣul*' (issues or enquiries from *Uṣul*) is presented. This has been taken from the second book of Ibn Ḥazm's *magnum opus* of *fiqh* (jurisprudence), *al-Muḥalla bil'Athār*.[4] Together with the translated text, several explanatory footnotes have been added to provide, where appropriate, additional explanation and references. Ibn Ḥazm's primary work

---

[2] A. G. Chejne has an invaluable overview in English of the life and works of Ibn Ḥazm. His text, though now quite dated, also includes a good translation of Ibn Ḥazm's *Marātib al-Ulum* [Categorisation of (the branches) of Knowledge]. *See:* A. G. Chejne (1982), *Ibn Ḥazm*, (Chicago: Kazi Publications).

[3] See: Adam Sabra, 'Ibn Ḥazm's Literalism: A Critique of Islamic Legal Theory,' pp. 97/160 in *Ibn Ḥazm of Cordoba: The Life and Works of a Controversial Thinker*.

[4] The eighteen issues (or enquiries) covered are taken from *al-Muḥalla*, Vol. 1, pp. 72/89. Each individual reference is cited per chapter.

relating to *Uṣul* is *al-Iḥkām fi-Uṣul al-Aḥkām*, which is often rendered into English as 'Judgement on the Principles of Law.' The abridgment of the *Iḥkām* is the shorter summary text which is entitled: *al-Nubdtha al-Kāfiyah fi-Uṣul al-Aḥkām al-Deen.*

Like many terms within the Islamic sciences, presenting a single encompassing English equivalent word for key terms is not always possible. Writing in *The Search for God's Law,* Bernard Weiss provides a succinct summary explanation in English of the term '*uṣul*':

> An *aṣl* (singular of *uṣul*) is that upon which something else depends for its realisation (as a branch of a tree depends for its growth upon the tree's roots, to employ the metaphor the term conveys). In relation to *fiqh*, the term *uṣul* designates all those things that are required for the emergence of *fiqh*. It is often translated as "principles," although in my estimation "foundations" somewhat better conveys the sense of *uṣul*.[5]

Explaining the construction of the phrase to that of *fiqh*, Muḥammad Shawkāni wrote in *Irshād al-Faḥul*: 'As for the construction to it, it is termed '*fiqh*', in the language it is: understanding. In (legal) terminology, it is *'ilm* (knowledge) of *al-Aḥkām al-Sharī'ah* (the legal rulings) that are extracted from the detailed evidences.'

These key issues of *Uṣul* are utilised throughout that work and are a feature of Ibn Ḥazm's unique legal method. Many of

---

[5] Bernard G. Weiss (2010), *The Search for God's Law: Islamic Jurisprudence in the writings of Sayf al-Din al-Amidi*, p. 25. In *al-Iḥkām fi-Uṣul al-Aḥkām*, al-'Amidi explains: '*Uṣul al-Fiqh* is the evidential indicators and approach upon which *fiqh* (jurisprudence) is built, functioning as evidences of *al-Aḥkām al-Sharī'ah* (the legal rulings) and how it is established from that formulation.'

these principles are though significant in themselves, not least because they provide a lucid empowering framework with which to approach some of the intractable debates that currently beset contemporary Islamic discourse.

For the updated edition of this text, we have tried to utilise a single-translation of the Qur'ān throughout. In this regard, the translation is that produced by Professor M. A. S Abdel Haleem.[6] Mainly this is for ease of reading, but also to try and ensure, as far as it practically possible, that there is a level of consistency to the translated meaning of each verse as it appears in context. On occasion, some of the quoted verses are expanded to provide greater contextual clarity.

K M Hasan
London, August 2022

---

[6] *The Qur'an* (2008), A new translation by Professor M. A. S Abdel Haleem, Oxford World Classics, (Oxford University Press: Oxford)

‘We blame our time, though we are to blame
No fault has time but only us
We scold the time for all the shame,
Had it a tongue it would scold us.’

[Muḥammad ibn Idris, Imām al-Shāfi’i]

1. The *Deen* of Islam is only to be taken from the Qur'ān or from the *Sunnah*

The *Deen* of Islam, which is necessary for everyone, can only be taken from the Qur'ān or from what was authentically reported on the authority of the Messenger of Allah peace and blessings be upon him.[7] Either with all the scholarly transmission from him (peace be upon him) and it is *al-Ijmā'* (consensus) and with textual concurrence from him (peace be upon him) and it is all textual. And either with the transmission of trustworthy narrators one from another until it reaches him (peace be upon him) and no more. The Exalted has said:

وَمَا يَنْطِقُ عَنِ الْهَوَى إنْ هُوَ إلا وَحْيٌ يُوحَى

Nor does he speak out of desire; it is naught but revelation that is revealed.[8]

اتَّبِعُوا مَا أُنزِلَ إِلَيْكُم مِّن رَّبِّكُمْ وَلَا تَتَّبِعُوا مِن دُونِهِ أَوْلِيَا

[7] No. 92, *al-Muḥalla*, Vol. 1, p. 72
[8] *Qur'ān*, 53: 3/4

Follow what has been sent down to you from your Lord; do not follow other masters beside Him.[9]

الْيَوْمَ أَكْمَلْتُ لَكُمْ دِينَكُمْ

Today I have completed your Deen. [10]

As opposed to the one who sees two verses or two authentic *ḥadith*, or (a singular) *Ṣaḥīḥ ḥadith* and verse, it is an obligation to utilise all of them, because obedience to each of them alike is obliged. It is not permissible to leave either one or the other, as long as we are capable thereof. And this is not to exclude the least meaning from that meaning of the vast majority. If we are not able to do that, then we must take the addition into the ruling, because it is certain that it is obligatory. It is not permissible to leave certitude for that which is guesswork. Neither is there discrepancy in the *Deen* or between Allah the Almighty and his *Deen*. For the Almighty has said:

الْيَوْمَ أَكْمَلْتُ لَكُمْ دِينَكُمْ

Today I have completed your Deen. [11]

وَنَزَّلْنَا عَلَيْكَ الْكِتَابَ تِبْيَانًا لِّكُلِّ شَىْءٍ

We revealed the Book to you explaining clearly everything.[12]

---

[9] *Qur'ān*, 7: 3. The full verse is quoted here, with the highlighting relating to the portion of the verse that Ibn Ḥazm utilises as the citation. The same highlighting will appear for other verses quoted where applicable.
[10] *Qur'ān*, 5: 3. Given the length of the verse, only the cited portion is presented here.
[11] Ibid.
[12] *Qur'ān*, 16: 89

2. The *ḥadith mawquf* and *mursal* do not establish proof by themselves

The *mawquf,*[13] and *mursal*, do not establish by themselves proof. And like that, no one narrates it, except those that are not trustworthy in relation to their *Deen* and their memorisation.[14] It is not lawful to leave (or abandon) what has come in the Qur'ān or that which is authentic from the Messenger of Allah peace be upon him, for the speech of a Companion or other than them. Whether it is the narrator of a *ḥadith* or it isn't, and the *mursal* is (containing) an (omitted) narrator between it, or between the

[13] The definition of the *mawquf* (halted) that is provided by Ibn Ṣalāḥ is as follows: 'The *mawquf ḥadith* is the one which is transmitted from the companions, may Allah be pleased with them, concerning their words, deeds and the like and which is stopped at them and is not carried past to the Messenger of Allah peace be upon him. If its *isnād* is cohesive to the companion, it is called 'connected halted' (*al-mawquf al-mawṣul*); and, if its *isnād* is not cohesive, it is called 'unconnected halted' (*al-mawquf ghayr al-mawsul*)...If the term 'halted' is used without any qualification, it refers exclusively...to a *ḥadith* of a companion.' See: Ibn Ṣalāḥ, *An Introduction of the Science of Ḥadith* [*Kitāb Ma'rifa Anwā' Ulum al-ḥadith*], translated by Dr. Eerik Dickinson (Reading: Garnet Publishing), 2006. The citation taken from p.33 has been slightly modified.

[14] No. 93, *al-Muḥalla*, Vol. 1, pp. 72/74

narrator and the Prophet peace be upon him.[15] The *mawquf* is not known as being that which reaches (its line of transmission) to the Prophet peace be upon him. Concerning the proof relating to the invalidity of the *mawquf*, the speech of Allah the Exalted (is):

رُّسُلًا مُّبَشِّرِينَ وَمُنذِرِينَ لِئَلَّا يَكُونَ لِلنَّاسِ عَلَى اللَّهِ حُجَّةٌ بَعْدَ الرُّسُلِ

They were messengers bearing good news and warning, so that mankind would have no excuse before Allah.[16]

There is no proof to be established by anyone beside that of the Messenger of Allah peace and blessings be upon him. It is not permissible for anyone to ascribe that to the Messenger of Allah peace and blessings be upon him, because it is *dthan* (conjecture, assumption, guesswork). Indeed, (concerning *dthan*) the Almighty has said:

---

[15] By its very nature, the *mursal ḥadith* is considered *ḍaef* (weak) unless supported through other alternate or attesting lines of reporting. Writing in the introduction to his *Ṣaḥīḥ* [Vol. 1, ch. 6, p. 31], Imām Muslim said: 'Thus, they permit themselves to narrate *ḥadiths* from one another in this way (with) *Irsāl* (looseness) without having heard them directly. All authoritative scholars agree, as I do, that a *mursal* report is not valid as evidence. Because of all this I find myself in need of ascertaining that each narrator heard the *ḥadith* from the one he quotes.' Ibn Ṣalāḥ writes: 'The form of the *mursal* (loose) *ḥadith* about which there is no disagreement is the *ḥadith* of a *Tābi'i al-kabir* (early Follower), like 'Ubayd-Allah b. 'Adi b. al-Khayyār, Sa'eed b. al-Mussayib and those like them who met a number of the Companions and attended their classes – when he said, 'The Messenger of Allah (peace be upon him) said.' The common view is that all of the Followers, may Allah be pleased with them, are to be treated equally in that regard...Be aware that a *mursal ḥadith* is treated as if it were weak unless its source is established as sound by the relation of the text through another line of transmission…' See: Ibn Ṣalāḥ, *An Introduction of the Science of Ḥadith* [*Kitāb Ma'rifa Anwā' Ulum al-ḥadith*], pp. 39/40.

[16] *Qur'ān*, 4: 165

وَإِنَّ الظَّنَّ لَا يُغْنِي مِنَ الْحَقِّ شَيْئًا

Guesswork is of no value against the truth. [17]

The Almighty has said:

وَلَا تَقْفُ مَا لَيْسَ لَكَ بِهِ عِلْمٌ إِنَّ السَّمْعَ وَالْبَصَرَ وَالْفُؤَادَ كُلُّ أُولَٰئِكَ كَانَ عَنْهُ مَسْئُولًا

Do not follow blindly what you do not know to be true: ears, eyes, and heart, you will be questioned about all these. [18]

As for the *mursal* and that which relates to its narrators, (it is) those that are not trustworthy in relation to their *Deen* and their memorisation and since Allah the Almighty says:

فَلَوْلَا نَفَرَ مِن كُلِّ فِرْقَةٍ مِّنْهُمْ طَائِفَةٌ لِّيَتَفَقَّهُوا فِي الدِّينِ وَلِيُنذِرُوا قَوْمَهُمْ إِذَا رَجَعُوا إِلَيْهِمْ

Out of each community, a group should go out to gain understanding of the Deen, so that they can teach their people when they return. [19]

It has been obliged to accept what the Almighty has proscribed concerning the application of understanding in *Deen*. He says:

يَا أَيُّهَا الَّذِينَ آمَنُوا إِن جَاءَكُمْ فَاسِقٌ بِنَبَإٍ فَتَبَيَّنُوا أَن تُصِيبُوا قَوْمًا بِجَهَالَةٍ فَتُصْبِحُوا عَلَىٰ مَا فَعَلْتُمْ نَادِمِينَ

---

[17] *Qur'ān*, 53: 28
[18] *Qur'ān*, 17: 36
[19] *Qur'ān*, 9: 122

O you who believe! If a fāsiq comes to you with a report, verify it, lest you harm a people in ignorance then be sorry for what you have done.[20]

There is nothing in this world except for justice or corruption and the Almighty has prohibited upon us the acceptance of a report carried by an evil-doer. That which remains besides that, is justice, and it is correct that his report is that which we are obliged to accept.

As for the *majhul* (the unknown), we are not assured that they have the attribute of being upright and *thiqa* (trustworthy), which Allah the Almighty has obliged the acceptance of their transmission, and it is the understanding in the *Deen.* It is not permissible for us to accept the transmission until we are assured of his understanding in *Deen* and his memorisation and the narrators absence from *fisq* (evil-doing). With Allah the Almighty is all *tawfeeq*.

Not a single individual has differed (as to the fact) that the Messenger of Allah peace and blessings be upon him, sent messengers to all kingdoms; a single messenger (sent) to each kingdom to call them unto Islam. One by one they were sent to every city and tribe, such as to Ṣanā', Najd, Haḍramawt, Taymā, Najrān, Bahrain, Oman and other than them. (This messenger) taught all of them the *aḥkām* (legal rulings) of the *Deen,* with that transmission being accepted by their teacher and leader. Hence it is correct to accept the *khabr al-wāḥid* (single-narrator report) being conveyed from one trustworthy narrator reporting the message from another unto the Messenger of Allah peace be upon him.

---

[20] *Qur'ān*, 49: 6

Whoever leaves the Qur'ān or what is authentic from the Messenger of Allah peace and blessings be upon him for the statement of a Companion or other than them, it is likened to be such as that report or other than it, he would have abandoned what Allah the Exalted has commanded him to, by following the statement for which Allah the Exalted has neither ordered him with, or commanded obedience upon him to follow. (Indeed) this is contrary to the order of Allah the exalted; neither is it virtuous (or) an obligation that Allah has commanded *taqleed* to their statement or their interpretation, because Allah the Exalted hasn't ordered that.[21] But the obligation rests upon the reverence, love and acceptance of his report only (*sic*. the Messenger of Allah), because it is this that Allah the Almighty has indeed obliged.

---

[21] Often referred to in English as 'imitation.' Weiss (2010), p. 297 writes: 'al-'Amidi defines *taqleed* as – 'Adherence to the dictum of someone else without an authoritative basis [for doing so].' The literal meaning of *taqleed* is 'adornment with a necklace.' When one adheres to the dictum of someone else without being able to provide evidence that he is required to do so, one adorns or invests the other person with authority.' See also: al-'Amidi, *al-Iḥkām* [Vol. 4, p. 269].

3. The Qur'ān abrogates the Qur'ān and the *Sunnah* abrogates the *Sunnah*

The Qur'ān abrogates the Qur'ān and the *Sunnah* abrogates the *Sunnah*.[22] He the Almighty said of the Qur'ān:

مَا نَنْسَخْ مِنْ آيَةٍ أَوْ نُنْسِهَا نَأْتِ بِخَيْرٍ مِنْهَا أَوْ مِثْلِهَا

Any revelation We cause to be superseded or forgotten, We replace with something better or similar.[23]

And the Exalted has further said:

لِتُبَيِّنَ لِلنَّاسِ مَا نُزِّلَ إِلَيْهِمْ

So that you can explain to people what was sent for them.[24]

وَمَا يَنْطِقُ عَنِ الْهَوَى إِنْ هُوَ إِلا وَحْيٌ يُوحَى

---

[22] No. 94, *al-Muḥalla*, Vol. 1, p. 74
[23] *Qur'ān*, 2: 106
[24] *Qur'ān*, 16: 44

Nor does he speak out of desire; it is naught but revelation that is revealed.[25]

And the Exalted commanded him (the Prophet) to say:

إِنْ أَتَّبِعُ إِلاَّ مَا يُوحَىٰ إِلَيَّ

I only follow what is revealed to me.[26]

And He the Exalted has said:

وَلَوْ تَقَوَّلَ عَلَيْنَا بَعْضَ الْأَقَاوِيلِ، لَأَخَذْنَا مِنْهُ بِالْيَمِينِ، ثُمَّ لَقَطَعْنَا مِنْهُ الْوَتِينَ، فَمَا مِنكُم مِّنْ أَحَدٍ عَنْهُ حَاجِزِينَ

If [the Prophet] had attributed some fabrication to Us, We would certainly have seized his right hand and cut off his lifeblood, and none of you could have defended him.[27]

All of what the Messenger of Allah peace and blessings be upon him said is true, he said that it is from Allah the Exalted. Some of that declared *bayān* was abrogated and all of that, is from Allah the Exalted.

---

[25] *Qur'ān*, 53: 3/4
[26] *Qur'ān*, 6: 50
[27] *Qur'ān*, 69: 44/47

4. Abrogation and specification in the Qur'ān & the *Sunnah*

It is not permissible for anyone to say regarding any verse of the Qur'ān or a statement of the Messenger of Allah, may the peace and blessings of Allah be upon him, with an assertion: this is *mansukh* (abrogated) and this is *makhṣuṣ* (restricted, specified) as a logical necessity or due to the apparent nature of its wording.[28] Neither can they say that the text is allegorical, or that the ruling extracted from the text doesn't constitute an obligation due to circumstance, except with another text which makes clear what the circumstances are as mentioned, a total and certain agreement that the text is to be understood as such, or by rational necessity. If the above conditions are not met, then the claimant is a liar. The proof for that, is the speech of Allah the Exalted and Majestic:

وَمَا أَرْسَلْنَا مِن رَّسُولٍ إِلَّا لِيُطَاعَ بِإِذْنِ اللَّهِ

[28] No. 95, *al-Muḥalla*, Vol. 1, pp. 74/75

All the Messengers We sent were meant to be obeyed, by Allah's leave.[29]

وَمَا أَرْسَلْنَا مِن رَّسُولٍ إِلَّا بِلِسَانِ قَوْمِهِ لِيُبَيِّنَ لَهُمْ

We have never sent a messenger who did not use his own people's language to make things clear for them.[30]

بِلِسَانٍ عَرَبِيٍّ مُّبِينٍ

In plain Arabic language. [31]

وَقَدْ كَانَ فَرِيقٌ مِّنْهُمْ يَسْمَعُونَ كَلَامَ اللَّهِ ثُمَّ يُحَرِّفُونَهُ مِن بَعْدِ مَا عَقَلُوهُ

Some of them used to hear the words of Allah and then deliberately twist them, even when they understood them.[32]

فَلْيَحْذَرِ الَّذِينَ يُخَالِفُونَ عَنْ أَمْرِهِ أَن تُصِيبَهُمْ فِتْنَةٌ أَوْ يُصِيبَهُمْ عَذَابٌ أَلِيمٌ

And those who go against his order should beware lest a trial afflict them or they receive a painful punishment.[33]

As for the statement of the Almighty, He says:[34]

وَمَا أَرْسَلْنَا مِن رَّسُولٍ إِلَّا لِيُطَاعَ بِإِذْنِ اللَّهِ

---

[29] *Qur'ān*, 4: 64
[30] *Qur'ān*, 14: 4
[31] *Qur'ān*, 26: 195
[32] *Qur'ān*, 2: 75
[33] *Qur'ān*, 24: 63
[34] Repeating the first verse that was quoted

All the Messengers We sent were meant to be obeyed, by Allah's leave.[35]

The obligation is to obey the Messenger of Allah peace be upon him regarding everything that was ordered by him, and the speech of the Exalted says: '*Say: Obey Allah and the Messenger...*'[36] which establishes the obligation of obeying the Qur'ān, and whomsoever calls unto a verse or a *khabr* (report) that is abrogated, the obligation of obedience to them in that falls away, as that is contrary to the command of Allah in that. The Exalted says:

وَمَا أَرْسَلْنَا مِن رَّسُولٍ إِلَّا بِلِسَانِ قَوْمِهِ لِيُبَيِّنَ لَهُمْ

We have never sent a messenger who did not use his own people's language to make things clear for them.[37]

It is essential to take a text in the Qur'ān and the reports on the necessary and obvious meanings. Whomsoever takes a text to be understood in a manner that is not necessitated in the Arabic language, in a befitting manner, he has fallen short in understanding the text and has a false understanding. This is a statement against Allah that is false, and includes taking part of the implications of the text, while leaving the rest. He the Exalted said:

فَلْيَحْذَرِ الَّذِينَ يُخَالِفُونَ عَنْ أَمْرِهِ

---

[35] *Qur'ān*, 4: 64
[36] *Qur'ān*, 3: 32
[37] *Qur'ān*, 14: 4

And those who go against his order should beware. [38]

This is a warning against the one who claims it is not upon them to agree with His command, when all the text indicate that it is an obligation. As for the one who claims the obligation can be delayed for a time, he has also fallen short in the obligation of obeying Allah, and what was obligated by Him in obeying the Messenger peace be upon him, in the time-period of the delay. All of this is in opposition to the command of Allah, lord of majesty and honour. The text of the Qur'ān or the *Sunnah* of the Messenger, constitute an obligation, except with the qualifications we have mentioned above, such as by consensus, or another authentic text, or by rational necessity. Such a claimant's statement would be correct; Allah's command must be obeyed. As for one who, by logical necessity, (does this by) his desire, then their call is one to the destruction of Islam, as well as all that is established by the (branches of) knowledge, and of language and this is indeed corruption.

And unto Allah is all *tawfeeq*.

---

[38] *Qur'ān*, 24: 63

5. Consensus is that which we are certain all the Companions of the Messenger of Allah knew

The *Ijmā'* (consensus) is that of which we are certain that all of the *Ṣaḥāba* (Companions) of the Messenger of Allah peace and blessings be upon him knew of.[39] And they all have said the same without any of them differing, may Allah be pleased with them all. Like our certainty that they all prayed with him (peace be upon him) the five-daily-prayers with this (requisite) number of bows and prostrations, or that they knew that he prayed with the people in that manner. Or that they all fasted with him and that he fasted (the month of) *Ramaḍān* with the people (while resident).

This is similar to all other legal obligations upon which we are certain of. Those who do not believe in such legal obligations / prohibitions are not considered to be one of the believers. No one has disagreed that there is *ijmā'* upon such matters. At that time, the *Ṣaḥāba* were the only believers on earth, with none other beside them. Whoever claims anything else is *ijmā'* besides this, then it would be incumbent upon them to bring forth

---

[39] No. 96, *al-Muḥalla*, Vol. 1, pp. 75/76

evidence to substantiate such a position and he will not be able to do so to show it is valid and binding.

6. What is not consensus

And if there is any issue where there is an established disagreement amongst any one of them (the Companions) may Allah be pleased with them, or we are not certain that all have agreed upon it, or we have evidence that one has disagreed, then it is not *ijmā'*.[40] Whoever has claimed that there is *ijmā'* here is lying and indeed he has no knowledge of it, as Allah the Almighty has said:

وَلَا تَقْفُ مَا لَيْسَ لَكَ بِهِ عِلْمٌ إِنَّ السَّمْعَ وَالْبَصَرَ وَالْفُؤَادَ كُلُّ أُولَٰئِكَ كَانَ عَنْهُ مَسْئُولًا

Do not follow blindly what you do not know to be true: ears, eyes, and heart, you will be questioned about all these. [41]

[40] No. 97, *al-Muḥalla*, Vol. 1, p. 76
[41] *Qur'ān*, 17: 36

7. It is not permissible that all people of a given generation can agree upon a mistake

The *jmā'* (consensus) of the people of a given era after them, the first to the last, concerning the ruling upon a text - that does not sever the consensus of the Companions.[42] Even if it is possible to be certain regarding the *ijmā'* of the people of a given era, the first to the last of them, concerning the ruling upon a text, that doesn't sever the consensus of the Companions, may Allah be pleased with them. With that severance, it is truth and a proof, but it is not a *ijmā'*. As for its severance, it is a proof and truth, as we have mentioned previously with the *isnād* from the statement of the Messenger of Allah peace and blessings be upon him:

لَنْ تَزَالَ طَائِفَةٌ مِنْ أُمَّتِي ظَاهِرَةً عَلَى الْحَقِّ لَا يَضُرُّهُمْ مَنْ خَذَلَهُمْ حَتَّى يَأْتِيَ أَمْرُ اللهِ

'A group of people from my Ummah will always remain triumphant on the right path and continue to be triumphant. He who deserts

[42] No. 98, *al-Muḥalla*, Vol. 1, pp. 76/77

them shall not be able to do them any harm. They will remain in this position until Allah's command is executed.'[43]

It is authentic from this, that it is absolutely not permissible for the people of a given era to gather upon a *khaṭā'* (mistake). It is necessary to speak the truth unto them, and that it is not consensus. The reason being, is that the people of each era after that generation of the companions – may Allah be pleased with them all – are not all the believers. Rather, they are some of the believers and the consensus is but the consensus of all the believers and not just some of them. If it were possible to call it a consensus, what has been is excluded from that, one doesn't know what the others have agreed upon, or what they have disagreed upon, therefore it isn't called a consensus, as those who have departed from that (could be) two, three or four. So, it never is called a consensus with what one has said. This is invalid. But there is no way to ascertain the consensus of the people of a given era *after* the companions - may Allah be pleased with them – like that. In fact, they were (the companions) a limited number, so it was possible to determine the statements they made concerning an issue. And with Allah is all *tawfeeq*.

Some of the people have said, that the matter (*ijmā'*) is known by where there is approval from the followers of Mālik, Shāfi'i and Abu Ḥanifah; if they approve that point of view. Ali (Ibn Ḥazm) said: yet this is a mistake since there is no way of knowing that within that given issue these followers have all

---

[43] Ibn Ḥazm only quotes the *matn* (text) of the narration here as it is quoted in full elsewhere. The full *isnād* as recorded by Imām Muslim in the book of government is: Sa'eed ibn Manṣur, Abu al-Rabih' al-Ataki and Qutayba ibn Sa'eed narrated to us, they said: Ḥammād and he is Ibn Zayd narrated to us from Ayub from Abu Qilābah from Abu Usāmah from Thawbān, he said the Messenger of Allah peace be upon him said.

agreed; that one of the scholars has not dissented concerning that, while agreeing with the remainder of his sayings.

8. Disagreements of the people or the dissent of one in relation to an issue

If the people disagree upon a matter or there is dissent concerning an issue, it is obligatory to refer that matter to the Qur'ān and the *Sunnah* of the Messenger of Allah peace and blessings be upon him – and not to anything other than that.[44] It is not permissible to refer to the acts of the people of Medina or any other than that. The proof for that is what Allah the Exalted and Majestic has said:

يَا أَيُّهَا الَّذِينَ آمَنُوا أَطِيعُوا اللَّهَ وَأَطِيعُوا الرَّسُولَ وَأُولِي الْأَمْرِ مِنكُمْ فَإِن تَنَازَعْتُمْ فِي شَيْءٍ فَرُدُّوهُ إِلَى اللَّهِ وَالرَّسُولِ إِن كُنتُمْ تُؤْمِنُونَ بِاللَّهِ وَالْيَوْمِ الْآخِرِ

O you who believe! Obey Allah and obey the Messenger and those in authority from amongst you; then if you differ about anything, refer it to Allah and the Messenger, if you believe in Allah and the last day.[45]

[44] No. 99, *al-Muḥalla*, Vol. 1, pp. 77/78

[45] *Qur'ān*, 4: 59. Only the latter tail-end of the verse is cited in the Arabic text, but the full verse is included here for the sake of completeness.

It is well established in the matters of dispute that it is only referred to the words of Allah and the *Sunnah* of the Messenger of Allah peace and blessings be upon him. In this there is a prohibition of referring to the speech of others beside the Messenger of Allah peace and blessings be upon him. (This is) because whoever refers to the speech of mankind, besides he, peace and blessings be upon him, would have violated the express command of Allah the Exalted, where he ordered to return the matter to him and His Messenger, especially given that he has linked that with the wording: '*if you believe in Allah and the last day.*'[46] Allah the Exalted did not issue an order to refer to the statements of *some* of the believers besides all others. And with Allah is all *tawfeeq*.

And indeed, the *Khulafā'* (pl. *Khalif*) – may Allah be pleased with them, like Abu Bakr, Umar and Uthmān were in Medina; some of them were in Yemen and Mecca. Others were sent as governors by Umar to Baṣra, Kufa, Egypt and Shām. It is impossible to believe that they, may Allah be pleased with them, would have left the knowledge from all other places concerning the obligated, the *ḥalāl* and the *ḥarām* only in Medina, that is falsehood – it is a bad attribute and may Allah protect them from that. Moreover, the kings of Bani Umayah dropped some *takbirs* from the prayer and performed the *khuṭba* before the Eid prayer until that bad habit became widespread over the lands. So it is correct that reference to the acts of others besides the Messenger of Allah peace and blessings be upon him, are not constituting an authority (or binding) proof.

---

[46] Ibid.

9. Analogy

It is not lawful to use the sayings of *Qiyās* (analogy) in the matters of *Deen* or in *Ra'i* (opinion) because of the command of Allah the Exalted has come to refer matters of dispute back to His book and His Messenger peace and blessings be upon him, and this is well established.[47] It is true, that to refer to *Qiyās* or an *illah*[48] or some reasoning or to an opinion, that is disputing with the command of Allah the Exalted as he has connected the matter with *'Imān* (faith). It is a referral to other than the command of Allah the exalted and this is the matter of it. Ali said: and Allah the Exalted has said:

مَا فَرَّطْنَا فِي الْكِتَابِ مِنْ شَيْءٍ

We have missed nothing out of the Book.[49]

وَنَزَّلْنَا عَلَيْكَ الْكِتَابَ تِبْيَانًا لِّكُلِّ شَيْءٍ وَهُدًى وَرَحْمَةً وَبُشْرَىٰ لِلْمُسْلِمِينَ

---

[47] No. 100, *al-Muḥalla*, Vol. 1, pp. 78/84

[48] An underlying reason or effective cause

[49] *Qur'ān*, 6: 38

For We have sent the Scripture down to you explaining everything, and as guidance, mercy and good news to those who devote themselves to Allah.[50]

لِتُبَيِّنَ لِلنَّاسِ مَا نُزِّلَ إِلَيْهِمْ

So that you can explain to people what was sent for them.[51]

الْيَوْمَ أَكْمَلْتُ لَكُمْ دِينَكُمْ

Today I have completed your Deen. [52]

These (verses) implicate and entail the annihilation of *Qiyās* and *Ra'i*, because all the people of *Qiyās* and *Ra'i* are agreed that it is not lawful to utilise them when there is a text. Indeed, Allah the Exalted testifies that *the text has not neglected anything* and that the Messenger of Allah peace and blessings be upon him, expounded to the people all that was revealed upon them. It is well established that the text encompasses all the *Deen*. Hence if that is so, there is no need for anyone to resort to *Qiyās* or unto *Ra'i* or an *illah* of *Ra'i* or anything other than that.

Furthermore, we would ask those who say by *Qiyās*, is every *Qiyās* which one who undertakes, is it all true or is some of it true and some of it false? If they say that all of it is true, then that is impossible, because we know there are various analogies that bring contradictory findings, may Allah protect us from that. What is the measure by which we can distinguish between the

[50] *Qur'ān*, 16: 89
[51] *Qur'ān*, 16: 44
[52] *Qur'ān*, 5: 3

ḥaqq (truth) and *bātil* (falsehood) as it relates to *Qiyās*? But we do show you that your attestation regarding accepting *Qiyās* as correct demonstrates the corruption contained within your analogies. There is no saying that has been shown falsehood by saying that he has lied himself. Indeed, the text of the Exalted is upon this, as He has said:

وَقَالَتِ الْيَهُودُ وَالنَّصَارَىٰ نَحْنُ أَبْنَاءُ اللَّهِ وَأَحِبَّاؤُهُ قُلْ فَلِمَ يُعَذِّبُكُم بِذُنُوبِكُم

The Jews and the Christians say, 'We are the children of God and His beloved ones.' Say: 'Then why does He punish you for your sins?[53]

If it is said, all *Qiyās* can become truth because analogies are in actuality mutually exclusive, and it is impossible for the thing to be opposed to both prohibition and that which is lawful. And this isn't where there is a place for *naskh* (abrogation) and neither *takṣiṣ* (specification). Like the reports that are conflicting which abrogate each other, and specify one another. If it is said from it (there is) truth and from it void. It (would be) said to him, we knew with what is known the authentic *Qiyās* from that which is *fasād* (corrupted) - there is no way for them to ever find that. If there is no evidence found upon the correct authentic (matter) from *Qiyās* from the void among it. Yet indeed, all of it is void and it has become a claim without proof. If they (were to) claim that *Qiyās* is ordered by Allah the exalted, it is asked, where have they found that? If they say, Allah the exalted and majestic has said:

فَاعْتَبِرُوا يَا أُولِي الْأَبْصَارِ

---

[53] *Qur'ān*, 5: 18

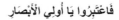

Learn from this, all of you with insight![54]

It is said unto them that the word, *al-'Itibār* (الإعْتِبَار) is not in the vernacular of the Arabs, and revealed Qur'ān except in relation to wonderment. Allah the Exalted has said:

وَإِنَّ لَكُمْ فِي الْأَنْعَامِ لَعِبْرَةً نُّسْقِيكُم مِّمَّا فِي بُطُونِهِ مِن بَيْنِ فَرْثٍ وَدَمٍ لَّبَنًا خَالِصًا سَائِغًا لِّلشَّارِبِينَ

In livestock, too, you have a lesson - We give you a drink from the contents of their bellies, between waste matter and blood, pure milk, sweet to the drinker. [55]

لَقَدْ كَانَ فِي قَصَصِهِمْ عِبْرَةٌ لِّأُولِي الْأَلْبَابِ مَا كَانَ حَدِيثًا يُفْتَرَىٰ وَلَٰكِن تَصْدِيقَ الَّذِي بَيْنَ يَدَيْهِ وَتَفْصِيلَ كُلِّ شَيْءٍ وَهُدًى وَرَحْمَةً لِّقَوْمٍ يُؤْمِنُونَ

There is a lesson in the stories of such people for those who understand. This revelation is no fabrication: it is a confirmation of the truth of what was sent before it; an explanation of everything; a guide and a blessing for those who believe.[56]

(The meaning of) which is to wonder, from being amazed. It is incredulous to say that the word *'Itibār* relating to wonderment and being amazed, could be inferred to mean that it relates to *Qiyās*. It is not correct that Allah would say to us to do *Qiyās* (to make analogies) then not expound and explain to us what that is (precisely); how is it to be done and what we are making analogy of. This is not possible because it is not possible for anyone to know anything concerning the *Deen* except by the teaching of

---

[54] *Qur'ān*, 59: 2
[55] *Qur'ān*, 16: 66
[56] *Qur'ān*, 12: 111

Allah the exalted to him by way of the tongue of the Messenger of Allah peace be upon him. Indeed, Allah the Exalted says:

لا يُكَلِّفُ اللَّهُ نَفْسًا إلا وُسْعَهَا

Allah does not burden any soul with more than it can bear. [57]

Should they mention certain *aḥādith* and verses in which something is likened to something, and that Allah has judged and decreed with an order like that, we would say to them: all that which Allah the exalted and the Messenger peace be upon him said from that, indeed it is truth, it is the *naṣṣ* (text). It is not lawful for anyone to disagree with it as it is text and with that we say - wherever they claim they can compare and make analogy where there isn't a reason for that, then it is outside of the text, so we don't invent that, so it must be false and creating a new *Sharī'ah* that Allah didn't permit. All that you want to resemble in *Deen* and explain that which is not stated by Allah or His Messenger peace be upon him is void and creating a *Sharī'ah* that Allah the exalted did not sanction.

And this falsifies their claims, the mention of the verse relating to hunting (whilst in pilgrimage) also invalidates their claims, and '*What do you think if you rinse your mouth with water while you are fasting?*' [58] as well as -

---

[57] *Qur'ān*, 2: 286

[58] Only a portion of the narration is cited. Abu Dāwud records this in his *Sunan* in the book of fasting. The full text reads: Ahmad ibn Yunus narrated to us al-Layth narrated to us *ḥawala* Esa ibn Ḥammād narrated to us, al-Layth ibn Sa'd reported to us from Bukeer ibn Abdullah from Abdal-Malik ibn Sa'eed from Jābir ibn Abdullah he said, Umar ibn al-Khaṭṭāb said: I got excited, so I kissed while I was fasting, I then said: Messenger of Allah, I have done a big deed; I kissed while I was fasting. He said: '*What do you think if you rinse your mouth with water while you are fasting*?' In his *ḥadith,* Esa ibn Ḥammād said: There is no harm in it.

مِنْ أَجْلِ ذَٰلِكَ كَتَبْنَا عَلَىٰ بَنِي إِسْرَائِيلَ

On account of [his deed], We decreed to the Children of Israel.[59]

For indeed, every verse and *hadith* that they have brought forth (to justify their arguments) is marshalled against them and it is with that, the proofs are established against them, such as developed in the book: *al-Iḥkām fi-Uṣul al-Aḥkām,*[60] and in the books of *al-Nukkat,*[61] *al-Durra,*[62] and *Nubdtha.*[63]

Ali said: we have opposed every one of their analogies with one that is similar for like or better, which will come in detail, according to their principles of ruling, in order to show them the invalidity of *Qiyās* generally. And all what they have opposed us with (in retort), is that you have utilised *Qiyās* in order to undermine our *Qiyās*, like someone trying to use a rational argument to undermine reason.

Ali (Ibn Ḥazm) said: for we say that this is a very weak argument that is easy to undermine and unto Allah is all praise. We didn't use *Qiyās* to undermine *Qiyās*, but rather we have used *Qiyās* in order to show that its results are false from its very premise. There is no statement that is falser than one which falsifies itself. For indeed the text of the exalted is upon this, the exalted has said:

---

[59] *Qur'ān*, 5: 32
[60] Often rendered into English as 'Judgment on the Principles of Law,' this is Ibn Ḥazm's primary work relating to *Uṣul*.
[61] The full title of this work being: *al-Nukat al-mujaza fi nafy al-Ra'i wa-l-Qiyās wa-l-Ta'lil wal-'Itiqād.*
[62] *Kitāb al-Durra fimā yajib 'itiqādahu*
[63] *al-Nubdtha al-Kāfiyah fi-Uṣul al-Aḥkām al-Deen* is the short work which summarises the *Iḥkām*, op cit. In the introduction to this work, Ibn Ḥazm states that it is intended to be a short book that is easy to memorise and understand, which encapsulates the central arguments of the *Iḥkām*.

وَقَالَتِ الْيَهُودُ وَالنَّصَارَى نَحْنُ أَبْنَاءُ اللَّهِ وَأَحِبَّاؤُهُ قُلْ فَلِمَ يُعَذِّبُكُم بِذُنُوبِكُمْ

The Jews and the Christians say, 'We are the children of God and His beloved ones.' Say: 'Then why does He punish you for your sins?[64]

Allah did not approve their statements that they are his children and beloved, but even to assume that the statement is correct, why is the conclusion not the right one that we have? This is not like the people who use rational arguments to try and undermine reason, because from utilising the rational argument it approves the validity of reason, thereby undermining their own statements. There is no proof other than it has appeared invalid.

We have not resorted to *Qiyās* merely by using it but by demonstrating its invalidity by the textual and rational proofs. We explained that further we are not using *Qiyās* to undermine their *Qiyās* thereby arguing that our process of analogy is more correct. Rather, *all Qiyās* is deemed invalid, as they are contradictory and false. Our intention is to show that in principle it is invalid. Exactly as we have used against certain people that hold to a particular point of view, by utilising their own statements that they have testified upon in order to show they are incorrect such as from the Mutazilites, the Rāfiḍah, Murji'ah, Khawārij, (as well as) the Jews, Christians and (even) the atheists.

From their own statements, to which they witness are correct, so as to show them their internal corruptions and contradictions. And the same is done by you in your argumentation. Neither we nor you admit what the Jews and Christians say as a premise is correct. So, we say: let us assume

---

[64] *Qur'ān*, 5: 18

(for the moment) that its correct in order to show them the internal contradictions and inconsistencies. The same applies for you the people of *Qiyās*. We use their own books to undermine their own statements, not that we believe that their books are completely pure, but to show that there are internal contradictions.

Every legal school has a similar *Qiyās* to which a different view is reached. It is even clearer when we see that every group of them are arising in disagreements in any issue where they use *Qiyās*, one group will bring a *Qiyās* and another group a different one. And they agree that not all *Qiyās* is deemed to be valid, and not every point of view is correct (hence, what is the correct criterion to distinguish the correct point of view). Even in the case in which you can distinguish between the correct *Qiyās* and the incorrect *Qiyās*, and the correct and incorrect opinion, even in the case of '*illah* (reasoning) bring us the proper definition that can be used for *Qiyās* and not for *Qiyās*. When we asked them for this criterion, they were unable to provide an answer. They became silent, because they have none.

Ali (Ibn Ḥazm) said: and here is the place that if you press them upon these issues, it will show the invalidity and the falsehood of all their statements. They will not (be able) to come with an answer ever. If they bring a text then we say to them that the text is *ḥaqq* (true), but that which you are adding to that with your opinions is not, it is false, and will never be valid. They may claim that the companions, may Allah be pleased with them, agreed upon the matter of *Qiyās to be used*, it will be said to them – you have lied, and they have all unanimously agreed that it is falsehood and not to be used. The proof of that, is that they cannot find any *ḥadith* or *athār* narrated from the companions, may Allah be pleased with them, where it has been ordered generally to utilise *Qiyās* except in the falsified and fabricated epistle attributed to Umar may Allah be pleased with him, in which he is alleged to have said to: 'become acquainted with similarities and analogies. Thereafter compare the matter.'[65]

This epistle has only been narrated by Abdal-Malik ibn al-Waleed ibn Ma'dān from his father and he is *sāqiṭ* (fallen, as a narrator); his father is even worse than his son.[66] But even more so, how can they take this epistle to be an authority but they don't take the other parts of it where they have disagreed with Umar concerning it. For example, he says within it, all Muslims are just between each other except the one flogged in *ḥadd* or someone who is having a questionable allegiance or that of a questionable relation of belonging (nepotism), and all of them – all those who do *Qiyās* – Mālik, Shāfi'i and Abu Ḥanifah – do not adopt these statements of Umar.

So how is it that Umar is an authority in relation to saying make *Qiyās*, but at the same time not an authority in relation to

---

[65] An excerpt from the letter attributed to Umar setting out the instructions of the judge to Abu Musa al-Ashari. The sentence in full is: 'Pay attention to comprehending what revolves disturbingly in your chest that has no Qur'ān or *Sunnah* applicable to it, and become acquainted with similarities and analogies. Thereafter compare the matter; then have recourse to that which is most preferable to Allah and most in conformity of them to *ḥaqq* as you see.' *Sunan* al-Dāraquṭni [Vol. 4, no. 4425]. While the *isnād* of al-Dāraquṭni doesn't contain Abdal-Malik ibn al-Waleed ibn Ma'dān, it does however have 'Ubaydallah ibn Abi Ḥumayd, which is fatal. The print version of *Sunan* al-Dāraquṭni has this as being *ḍaef jiddan* (very weak). Al-Bukhāri and al-Nasā'i declared this narrator to be *munkar al-hadith*, others *ḍaef.* See Ibn Jawzi *al-Ḍu'afā' wa-l-Matrūkīn* [Vol. 2, no. 2236], al-Dāraquṭni *al-Ḍu'afā' wa-l-Matrūkīn* [no. 330, p. 117], and Ibn Ḥajar, *Tahzeeb* [Vol. 7, no. 17].

[66] In *al-Ḍu'afā al-Kabir* [Vol. 5, no. 1146], al-Uqayli records: 'Adam ibn Musa narrated to me he said I heard al-Bukhāri saying Abdal-Malik ibn al-Waleed ibn Ma'dān al-Ḍabi, *fihi nazar,'* which is Bukhāri's designation that the narrator is considered to be extremely weak. See also Ibn Ḥajar, *Tahzeeb* [Vol. 6, no. 796].

all Muslims are just between each other except the one flogged in *ḥadd* or someone who is having a questionable allegiance or that of a questionable relation of belonging (nepotism)? If it's a statement of Umar, if the epistle is correct, and *Qiyās* is an authority, then these latter points must also be held as an authority, but they do not adopt this.

The evidence that all the *Ṣaḥāba* have agreed that they shouldn't take *Ra'i* or *Qiyās*, is that nobody disagreed that all *Ṣaḥāba* believed in the Qur'ān and they read the following in:

الْيَوْمَ أَكْمَلْتُ لَكُمْ دِينَكُمْ

Today I have completed your Deen. [67]

فَإِن تَنَازَعْتُمْ فِي شَيْءٍ فَرُدُّوهُ إِلَى اللَّهِ وَالرَّسُولِ

Then if you differ about anything, refer it to Allah and the Messenger. [68]

So it's impossible that all of the *Ṣaḥāba* have agreed to neglect the Qur'ān and *Sunnah* in this regard and solely resort to *Ra'i* or *Qiyās*. Accusing them of such neglect is really a seriously grave matter. Moreover, it has been established that the Ṣadeeq (Abu Bakr) may Allah be pleased with him said: 'which earth would carry me or which heaven would cover me if I say in one of the verses of the book of Allah by mere opinion without firm knowledge.' And al-Fāruq (Umar) may Allah be pleased with him said: 'Distrust your opinion in *Deen*, indeed the opinion of us is *dthan* (guesswork) and conjecture.' From Uthmān may

---

[67] *Qur'ān*, 5: 3. Given the length of the verse, only the cited portion is presented here.
[68] *Qur'ān*, 4: 59

Allah be pleased with him, as he said in an edict, 'this was just an opinion of mine – either you may take it or leave it.'

And from Ali may Allah be pleased with him, 'If *Deen* were to be established by opinion and guesswork then wiping the *khuff* (socks) would be more reasonable than wiping on top of it.' From Sahl ibn Ḥunayf may Allah be pleased with him, 'O people, distrust your opinions in matters of your *Deen*.'[69] From Ibn 'Abbās may Allah be pleased with him, 'And whoever says (something) about the Qur'ān according to his (own) opinion, then let him take his seat in the fire.'[70] From Ibn Mas'ud may Allah be pleased with him, 'I will say in the exertion of my opinion, if it is right it is from Allah, but if its mistaken it is from myself and the *Shayṭān* and Allah and his Messenger are innocent of that.'[71] From Mu'ādth ibn Jabal in the *ḥadith*: 'He who invented words that are not from the Book of Allah the Almighty nor from the *Sunnah* of the Messenger of Allah peace be upon him; for you and him are in misguidance and innovation.'[72] Similar has been narrated from the companions, may Allah be pleased with them, in any opinion that they express, it's a point of view, in which they are offering an arbitration or an agreement between disputing parties, or cautiousness but never (made) compulsory upon any one.

In the *ḥadith* of Mu'ādth ibn Jabal concerning '*Ijtihād by Ra'i (opinion) and I shall spare no effort*,' this is not authentic,

---

[69] The quoted part of this statement can be found in the collections of *Ṣaḥīḥ* Bukhāri and *Ṣaḥīḥ* Muslim in several places, notably in the book of holding fast to the Qur'an and *Sunnah* (Bukhāri), and the book of *Jihād* (Muslim).

[70] Tirmidhi cites this statement, together with its expanded wording in several places in the chapters relating to *Tafsir* in his *Sunan*.

[71] Imām al-Nasā'i cites this statement, together with its expanded wording and context in his *Sunan* in the book of marriage.

[72] Abu Dāwud cites this tradition in his *Sunan* together with its full wording in the book of *Sunnah*.

because no one narrates this except the only one reporting it, al-Ḥārith ibn 'Amr, and he is *majhul* (unknown).[73] We do not know (of the identity) of the men from the people of Ḥoms (Syria), as he did not name them (in the reporting) from Mu'ādth.[74]

---

[73] In his commentary upon *Musnad* Aḥmad, Shu'ayb al-Arnā'uṭ states of this tradition and another cited: 'Its *isnād* is *ḍaef* due to the anonymity of "the companions of Mu'ādth" and the unknown status of al-Ḥārith ibn 'Amr.' Classical scholars were readily familiar with the significant problems the transmission for this tradition presents. In *al-Tārikh al-Kabir* [Vol. 2, no. 2449, p. 277], Imām al-Bukhāri said: 'al-Ḥārith ibn 'Amr ibn Akhi al-Mughira ibn Shu'ba al-Thaqafi from the companions of Mu'ādth, from Mu'ādth; Abu 'Awn narrating from him. It is not authentic, it is not known by other than this (*sic.* line of reporting); *mursal.*'

[74] Abu Dāwud records this narration in the book of judgements. Ḥafs ibn Umar narrated to us from Shu'ba from Abi 'Awn from al-Ḥārith ibn 'Amr ibn Akhi al-Mughira ibn Shu'ba from some of the people of Homs from the companions of Mu'ādth ibn Jabal, that when the Messenger of Allah peace be upon him intended to send Mu'ādth ibn Jabal to the Yemen, he asked: *How will you judge when the occasion of deciding a case arises?* He replied: I shall judge in accordance with the book of Allah. He asked: *If you don't find it in the book of Allah?* He replied: (then) with the *Sunnah* of the Messenger of Allah peace be upon him. He asked: *If you don't find it in the Sunnah of the Messenger of Allah or in the book of Allah?* He replied: (by) the *Ijtihād* of my opinion, sparing no effort. The Messenger of Allah peace be upon him then patted him on the chest and said: *Praise be to Allah Who has helped the Messenger of the Messenger of Allah to find something which pleases the Messenger of Allah.* Other scholars have cited this tradition, among them: *Musnad* Aḥmad [Vol. 5, no. 22114 and 22153], *Musnad* Abu Dāwud al-Ṭayālisi [Vol. 1, no. 560], *al-Sunan al-Kubra,* Bayhaqy [Vol. 10, 20339 and 20340], *al-Mu'jam al-Kabir*, al-Ṭabarāni [Vol. 20, no. 362] and the *Muṣṣanaf* of Ibn Abi Shayba [Vol. 7, no. 59].

We have discussed all the *aḥādith* in relation to this in our book mentioned previously (*al-Iḥkām*), and all praise is unto Allah.[75]

حدثنا أحمد بن قاسم حدثنا أبو قاسم بن محمد حدثنا جدي قاسم بن أصبغ أخبرنا محمد بن إسماعيل الترمذي حدثنا نعيم بن حماد أخبرنا عبد الله بن المبارك أخبرنا عيسى بن يونس بن أبي إسحاق السبيعي عن حريز بن عثمان عن عبد الرحمن بن جبير بن نفير عن أبيه عن عوف بن مالك الأشجعي قال قال رسول الله صلى الله عليه وسلم تفترق أمتي على بضع وسبعين فرقة أعظمهم فتنة على أمتي قوم يقيسون الأمور بآرائهم فيحلون الحرام ويحرمون الحلال

Aḥmad ibn Qāsim narrated to us Abu Qāsim ibn Muḥammad narrated to us, my grandfather Qāsim ibn Aṣbagh narrated to us Muḥammad ibn Ismā'il al-Tirmidhi reported to us Nu'aym ibn Ḥammād narrated to us Abdullah ibn al-Mubārak reported to us Esa ibn Yunus ibn Abu Isḥāq al-Sabee'i reported to us from Ḥureez ibn Uthmān from Abdar-Raḥman ibn Jubayr ibn Nufayr from his father from 'Auf ibn Mālik al-Ashja'ee he said the Messenger of Allah peace and blessings be upon him

[75] Ibn Ḥazm sets out greater reasoning for rejection in *al-Iḥkhām fi Uṣul al-Aḥkām* [Vol. 2, pp. 435/436], arguing that the narration is *sāqiṭ* (completely fallen) as it is cited only from this line of transmission: from an unknown narrator who is narrating from an unknown group of people. Hence, it is not lawful that such narrations can be taken. He describes the narration as a manifest lie as well as being an outright fabrication, because it is directly at odds with clearly established evidences, notably the following Qur'ānic verses: 5: 3, 6: 38, 16: 89 and 16: 44. He asks, how can such a narration which purportedly has the Messenger of Allah stating if you *don't find the guidance* in the Book of Allah and the *Sunnah*, be correct when the clearly established texts expressly state otherwise? Pronouncing judgment in *Deen* by opinion and claiming guidance cannot be found in the Book and the *Sunnah* - all of which Ibn Ḥazm declares as being a manifest lie without any doubt. After this he partially quotes from the authentic tradition as found in Bukhāri and Muslim, where the people will take as leaders the ignorant, who when consulted will give verdict without knowledge.

> said: *My Ummah will split into seventy plus sects, the most severe of them in fitnah of my Ummah are those who compare things to their opinion, making lawful the ḥarām and making unlawful the ḥalāl.*

Ali (Ibn Ḥazm) said: All the *Sharī'ah* is either a *farḍ* (obligation), which you become disobedient and punishable if you leave it, or a *ḥarām* (prohibition) which you are liable for punishment if you do; or *mubāḥ* (permissibility) for which there is no punishment or obligation. Of that there are three-sub groups, the *mandub* (recommended), which if you perform you gain an additional reward, or *makruh* (disliked) in which you get a reward if you leave but no punishment if you perform, or an absolute permissibility, with neither reproach or sin if you perform or leave it. Allah the Almighty says:

خَلَقَ لَكُم مَّا فِي الْأَرْضِ جَمِيعًا

It was He who created all that is on the earth for you.[76]

وَقَدْ فَصَّلَ لَكُم مَّا حَرَّمَ عَلَيْكُمْ

Allah has already fully explained what He has forbidden you.[77]

So it is well established that everything is permissible until we have a clear exposition in the Qur'ān or *Sunnah* regarding its (actual) prohibition.

حدثنا عبد الله بن يوسف حدثنا أحمد بن فتح حدثنا عبد الوهاب بن عيسى
حدثنا أحمد بن محمد حدثنا أحمد بن علي حدثنا مسلم بن الحجاج أخبرني

---

[76] *Qur'ān*, 2: 29
[77] *Qur'ān*, 6: 119

زهير بن حرب حدثنا يزيد بن هارون حدثنا الربيع بن مسلم القرشي عن محمد بن زياد عن أبي هريرة أن رسول الله صلى الله عليه وسلم خطب فقال أيها الناس إن الله قد فرض عليكم الحج فحجوا، فقال رجل أكل عام يا رسول الله؟ فسكت حتى أعادها ثلاثا، فقال رسول الله صلى الله عليه وسلم لو قلت نعم لوجبت ولما استطعتم، ذروني ما تركتكم، فإنما هلك من كان قبلكم بكثرة سؤالهم واختلافهم على أنبيائهم فإذا أمرتكم بشيء فأتوا منه ما استطعتم، وإذا نهيتكم عن شيء فدعوه

Abdullah ibn Yusuf narrated to us Aḥmad ibn Fatḥ narrated to us Abd-al Wāhab ibn Esa narrated to us Aḥmad ibn Muḥammad narrated to us Aḥmad ibn Ali narrated to us,[78] Muslim ibn al-Ḥajjāj narrated to us Zuhayr ibn Ḥarb reported to me Yazeed ibn Ḥārun narrated to us al-Rabeeh' ibn Muslim al-Qurayshi narrated to us from Muḥammad ibn Ziyād from Abu Hurayrah who said: Allah's Messenger (peace be upon him) addressed us and said: *O people, Allah has made Ḥajj obligatory for you; so, perform Ḥajj.* A man said: Messenger of Allah, and (is it to be performed) every year? He (the Prophet) kept quiet, and he repeated it three-times, whereupon Allah's Messenger (peace be upon him) said: *If I were to say yes, it would become obligatory and you would not be able to do it. Leave me with what I have left to you, for those who were before you were destroyed because of excessive questioning, and their opposition to their Prophets. So, when I command you to do anything, do it as much as it lies in your power and when I forbid you to do anything, then abandon it.*

---

[78] Ibn Ḥazm's *isnād* to Imām Muslim.

Ali (Ibn Ḥazm) said: This *ḥadith* has comprehensively established all the situations of ruling in relation to the *Deen*, from beginning to the end. It is clear what the Prophet has remained silent about, neither he has commanded nor prohibited it, then it is permissible. It is neither prohibited nor obligated. What he has ordered is a *farḍ* and what he has prohibited is *ḥarām* and what he has commanded us with we have to do it once unless there is evidence for an order of repetition. So, what then is the reason for *Ra'i* or *Qiyās* after that? We thank Allah for his great favour and blessings.

If they were to say, it is not permissible to say its *ḥarām* to use *Qiyās* unless that is you are able to bring forth a prohibition concerning that from the Qur'ān and the *Sunnah*. We would answer in reply to them: we have brought you the evidence that it isn't permissible, that Allah said in the issue of disputes to refer to the Qur'ān and the *Sunnah*, as Allah has said:

اتَّبِعُوا مَا أُنزِلَ إِلَيْكُم مِّن رَّبِّكُمْ وَلَا تَتَّبِعُوا مِن دُونِهِ أَوْلِيَاءَ

Follow what has been sent down to you from your Lord; do not follow other masters beside Him.[79]

And He the Exalted has said:

فَلا تَضْرِبُوا لِلَّهِ الأَمْثَالَ إِنَّ اللَّهَ يَعْلَمُ وَأَنْتُمْ لا تَعْلَمُونَ

So do not make up images about Allah: Allah knows and you do not.[80]

[79] *Qur'ān*, 7: 3
[80] *Qur'ān*, 16: 74

The *Qiyās* is nothing but striking likenesses (or examples) before Allah the exalted. Then it is said unto them further, if the Rāfiḍah opposed you in this and said, that it isn't permissible to argue that *ilhām* (inspiration, intuition) is invalidated or that following the footsteps of the Imām is invalidated until we find the prohibition of that in the *naṣṣ* (text). Or it is said unto you that of following a people in imitation concerning every matter (amongst) mankind; what is the (cause) of separation? Rather the truth (of the matter), is that it isn't permissible to say anything about Allah, that there is a prohibition, a lawfulness or obligation except by way of *naṣṣ* (text) only.

And with Allah the Exalted and Majestic is all *tawfeeq*.

10. Actions of the Prophet are not obligated except where accompanied with a clear statement of command

The acts of the Prophet peace and blessings be upon him are not deemed *farḍ* (obligated) per se except where they are explaining something that has been commanded previously; being accompanied with a clear statement of command, it is then an order.[81] Otherwise following him in all what he does is desirable. The proof relating to this is what we have mentioned earlier, (namely) that we are not in need of anything except what he has commanded us with or what he has prohibited us from. That which relates to silence, that is fallen aside, since that is pardoned. And the Exalted has said:

لَقَدْ كَانَ لَكُمْ فِي رَسُولِ اللَّهِ أُسْوَةٌ حَسَنَةٌ

Indeed, the Messenger of Allah is an excellent model. [82]

---

[81] No. 101, *al-Muḥalla*, Vol. 1, p. 84
[82] *Qur'ān*, 33: 21

11. *Sharī'ah* of the previous Prophets

It is not permissible to follow any *Sharī'ah* of a Prophet (that came) before our Prophet (Muḥammad), peace and blessings be upon him.[83] As the Exalted has said:

لِكُلٍّ جَعَلْنَا مِنكُمْ شِرْعَةً وَمِنْهَاجًا

We have assigned a law and a path to each of you.[84]

حدثنا أحمد بن محمد بن الجسور حدثنا وهب بن مسرة حدثنا محمد بن وضاح حدثنا أبو بكر بن أبي شيبة حدثنا هشيم أخبرنا سيار عن يزيد الفقير أخبرنا جابر بن عبد الله أن النبي صلى الله عليه وسلم قال أعطيت خمسا لم يعطهن أحد قبلي: نصرت بالرعب مسيرة شهر، وجعلت لي الأرض مسجدا وطهورا، فأيما رجل من أمتي أدركته الصلاة فليصل، وأحلت لي الغنائم ولم تحل لأحد قبلي، وأعطيت الشفاعة، وكان النبي يبعث إلى قومه خاصة وبعثت إلى الناس عامة

Aḥmad ibn Muḥammad ibn al-Jasour narrated to us Wahb ibn Massara narrated to us Muḥammad ibn

[83] No. 102, *al-Muḥalla*, Vol. 1, p. 84
[84] *Qur'ān*, 5: 48

> Waḍḍāḥ[85] narrated to us Abu Bakr ibn Abi Shayba narrated to us Hushaym narrated to us Sayyār reported to us from Yazeed al-Faqir, Jābir ibn Abdullah reported to us that the Prophet peace and blessings be upon him said: *I have been given five* (things) *that have not been given to anybody before me: I have been supported with horror for a distance of one month; the whole earth has been made a masjid and ṭahur* (purified / clean) *for me; anyone from my Ummah, man or woman, can pray wherever they are; the spoils of war have been permitted to me whereas they were not for previous nations; I have been given the intercession, and every previous Prophet has been sent to his own people whereas I have been sent to all of mankind.*[86]

Since these Messengers have been sent to their own specific people they are not addressing us – so how can their *Sharī'ah* apply or even be obligatory upon us? What makes our current *Sharī'ah* applicable is that we have been addressed with it. Whoever denies this, would therefore deny this *ḥadith* and the special *faḍeelah* (blessing) that has been given to Muḥammad peace and blessings be upon him.[87] Whoever says that the laws of the previous Prophets apply to us now given the advent of the Prophet Muḥammad (peace be upon him) who is sent to all of mankind is lying.

And with Allah is all success.

---

[85] Ibn Ḥazm's *isnād* to Abu Bakr ibn Abi Shayba

[86] *Muṣṣanaf* Ibn Abi Shayba, [Vol. 17, no. 32299]. The *ḥadith* is not only narrated by Jābir but by as many as seven or eight *Ṣaḥāba*. It is *mutawātir* and to be found in many collections, for example in Bukhāri, Muslim and others.

[87] In other words, being sent to all mankind abrogates all previous *Sharī'ah's*.

12. It is not permissible for anyone to imitate another, whether alive or dead

It is not permissible for anyone to undertake *Taqleed* to anyone else whether alive or dead and everyone is obliged to do as much *ijtihād* according to his level of capability.[88] Anyone asking about an issue of the *Deen* essentially wants to know what Allah has made obligatory in this *Deen.* So, it is obligatory upon him to ask - even if he is the most ignorant amongst all of mankind - whoever is the most knowledgeable about *Deen* in his area, which he can reach within a reasonable distance of travelling. When he is directed to that person he should ask his question. When he is given a solution or answer to the problem or provided with a *fatwa* (legal *responsa*), he must insist – *is that what Allah*

[88] No. 103, *al-Muḥalla*, Vol. 1, pp. 85/86. In the print version, Aḥmad Shākir has provided a footnote to the opening part of the sentence with a reference to a statement by the Companion, Abdullah ibn Mas'ud, may Allah be pleased with him. This is referenced from *Majmu' al-Zawā'id* by al-Haythami [Vol. 1, p. 180]: 'From Abdullah ibn Mas'ud, he said: None of you should make *taqleed* to another man with regards to his *Deen*. If he (the one being followed) believes, then he believers; if he disbelievers, then he (also) disbelieves. If you had to do *taqleed* to another, then take those who have passed away, for indeed those who are alive are not safe from *fitnah*.' He said (al-Haythami): 'It is narrated by al-Ṭabarāni in *al-Kabir*, and its men (narrators) are the men of *Ṣaḥīḥ*.'

and His Messenger have ordered? If the person who is being asked says yes, he should take that and apply it to the best of his ability. If he says no, 'it is my point of view', or 'it is *Qiyās*' or 'this is the statement of x, y, or z', or 'a companion of the Prophet said that or did it', or 'a *tabi'* or a *faqeeh*', or he remained silent or he rebuked him saying - 'why are you asking that?!'; or if he replies with 'I don't know' - then he is not allowed to follow him in this matter and he should ask someone else.

So even the common man, the layman, is required to find out from the community who is the most knowledgeable in *Deen*. Generally, people will reply it is x or y as this is a known matter in the community and not hidden completely. Then he should go and ask that individual the same question - *is that what Allah and His Messenger have ordered*? If he replies yes, then he is obliged to take it and follow that ruling / judgement to the best of his ability, until he is informed or he learns that the *mufti* was mistaken in that. Therefore, in summary the crucial questions that the common man must ask are as follows:

- *Who is most knowledgeable about this aspect of the Deen / Sharī'ah in this area?*
- *And secondly when approaching this person, he must ask: 'Is that what Allah and His Messenger have ordered?'*

That is the *ijtihād* that is required of the layman. The evidence for this position is as follows: Allah the Exalted and Majestic says –

يَا أَيُّهَا الَّذِينَ آمَنُوا أَطِيعُوا اللَّهَ وَأَطِيعُوا الرَّسُولَ وَأُولِي الْأَمْرِ مِنكُمْ فَإِن تَنَازَعْتُمْ فِي شَيْءٍ فَرُدُّوهُ إِلَى اللَّهِ وَالرَّسُولِ

O you who believe! Obey Allah and obey the Messenger and those in authority from amongst you; then if you differ about anything, refer it to Allah and the Messenger.[89]

Allah did not command us to obey some of 'those in authority' and leave some others. If you imitate a certain scholar then you have obeyed one to the neglect of another who has disagreed with him. So, he who obeys one and leaves the others, then he is not applying the verse correctly. If there is a dispute, then the reference and judgement is only to Allah and His Messenger, hence the formulation of the questions above. Everybody should insist upon this when asking a question. If it is said in response to what we have argued that Allah has said:

فَاسْأَلُوا أَهْلَ الذِّكْرِ إِن كُنتُمْ لَا تَعْلَمُونَ

You can ask the people of the dhikr if you do not know.[90]

And also, that He the Exalted has said:

فَلَوْلَا نَفَرَ مِن كُلِّ فِرْقَةٍ مِّنْهُمْ طَائِفَةٌ لِّيَتَفَقَّهُوا فِي الدِّينِ وَلِيُنذِرُوا قَوْمَهُمْ إِذَا رَجَعُوا إِلَيْهِمْ لَعَلَّهُمْ يَحْذَرُونَ

Out of each community, a group should go out to gain understanding of the Deen, so that they can teach their people when they return and so that they can guard themselves against evil.[91]

---

[89] *Qur'ān*, 4: 59

[90] *Qur'ān*, 16: 43. We have opted for a more literal translation of the verse, departing from Haleem here.

[91] *Qur'ān*, 9: 122

We would emphatically state yes, that is undoubtedly true and Allah has never commanded us to accept from those who go to study the *Deen* to ask about or accept their own point of view, that of their *Shaykh* or guesswork. He is required to ask about the *Deen* from Allah and His Messenger - and they are required to comply with this. The same applies for the people of *Dhikr* as said in the verse – it is to ask what the *Dhikr* (Qur'ān and *Sunnah*) has established from Allah, not a person's point of view or guesswork. We ask them – the people of *Dhikr*, because not everyone is from the people of *Dhikr*, but we only ask for what the *Deen* is, what Allah and His Messenger have said and require from us.

Whoever claims that *taqleed* is obligatory upon the common man, he has claimed falsehood and there is no text of the Qur'ān, *Sunnah*, *Ijmā'* or even *Qiyās* to support that. And what is like that is definitely *bāṭil,*[92] by the agreement of all Muslims. The evidence to prove that this point is false is where Allah has said:

وَقَالُوا رَبَّنَا إِنَّا أَطَعْنَا سَادَتَنَا وَكُبَرَاءَنَا فَأَضَلُّونَا السَّبِيلَا

And they will say 'Lord! We obeyed our masters and our chiefs, and they led us astray.'[93]

Ijtihād means putting the utmost effort in order to find what the ruling of the *Deen* is and by necessity we know that no Muslim can be called Muslim until he is absolutely certain that Allah is his lord and Muḥammad is the final Messenger. This cannot be

[92] Invalid, rejected
[93] *Qur'ān*, 33: 67. To comprehend the magnitude of this point one should also read the two verses either side of this – verses 66 and 68.

doubted. Anyone who enquires about an issue is asking about the ruling of Allah, precisely because he is a Muslim. So that is well established that the minimum we can expect from him is to ask: is that the ruling of Allah and His Messenger? And the mufti must reply. This line of reasoning is possible for all, even if one is a slave from the land of *Qaw Qu*![94]

[94] It is unclear what this land or city is that Ibn Ḥazm refers to. The closest thing given the context is that it is like the English expression – 'the back of beyond'.

13. Questions from laymen to the people of Deen

If the common man asks about who is the most knowledgeable in this area of *Deen* and is then directed to two individuals, one man of *ḥadith* the other of *Qiyās* (analogy) and *Ra'i* (opinion), then he should proceed to ask the man of *ḥadith*.[95] It is not permitted at all to ask the man of *Qiyās* and *Ra'i*. The evidence for that is where Allah the Exalted and Majestic says:

الْيَوْمَ أَكْمَلْتُ لَكُمْ دِينَكُمْ وَأَتْمَمْتُ عَلَيْكُمْ نِعْمَتِي وَرَضِيتُ لَكُمُ الْإِسْلَامَ دِينًا

Today I have perfected your Deen for you, completed My blessings upon you, and chosen as your Deen, Islam.[96]

وَأَنزَلْنَا إِلَيْكَ الذِّكْرَ لِتُبَيِّنَ لِلنَّاسِ مَا نُزِّلَ إِلَيْهِمْ

We have sent down the Dhikr to you so that you can explain to people what was sent for them.[97]

[95] No. 104, *al-Muḥalla*, Vol. 1, pp. 86/87
[96] *Qur'ān*, 5: 3
[97] *Qur'ān*, 16: 44

This is the *Deen* which is based upon truth. The one which is perfected and has been explained by Muḥammad, so it cannot be related to *Qiyās* and *Ra'i*; furthermore, this is the only *Deen* which is truth and it cannot be based upon *Qiyās* and *Ra'i* because that is based upon *dthan* (guesswork, doubt, suspicion, uncertainty) and all *dthan* is *bāṭil*!

حدثنا أحمد بن محمد بن الجسور حدثنا أحمد بن سعيد حدثنا ابن وضاح حدثنا يحيى بن يحيى حدثنا مالك عن أبي الزناد عن الأعرج عن أبي هريرة أن رسول الله صلى الله عليه وسلم قال إياكم والظن فإن الظن أكذب الحديث

Aḥmad ibn Muḥammad ibn al-Jasour narrated to us Aḥmad ibn Sa'eed ibn Waḍḍāḥ narrated to us[98] Yaḥya ibn Yaḥya narrated to us Mālik narrated to us from Abu Zinād from al-'Araj from Abu Hurayrah that the Messenger of Allah peace and blessings be upon him said: *Beware of al-dthan* (guesswork, doubt, suspicion, uncertainty). *Verily al-dthan is the most untrue speech.*[99]

حدثنا يونس بن عبد الله حدثنا يحيى بن مالك بن عائذ أخبرنا أبو عبد الله بن أبي حنيفة أخبرنا أبو جعفر أحمد بن محمد بن سلامة الطحاوي حدثنا يوسف بن يزيد القراطيسي أخبرنا سعيد بن منصور أخبرنا جرير بن عبد المجيد عن المغيرة بن مقسم عن الشعبي قال: السنة لم توضع بالمقاييس

Yunus ibn Abdullah narrated to us Yaḥya ibn Mālik ibn 'Aā-iz narrated to us Abu Abdullah ibn Abi Ḥanifah

[98] This is Ibn Ḥazm's *isnād* to the *Muwaṭṭā'* of Mālik
[99] *Muwaṭṭā',* Imām Mālik [Vol. 2, no. 1616]. Most collectors of *ḥadith* have recorded this narration including Bukhāri, Muslim, Abu Dāwud, Ibn Ḥibbān etc.

reported to us Abu Ja'far Aḥmad ibn Muḥammad ibn Salāma al-Ṭaḥāwi reported to us Yusuf ibn Yazeed al-Qarāteesi narrated to us Sa'eed ibn Manṣur reported to us Jarir ibn Abdul-Majeed reported to us from al-Mughira ibn Miqsam from al-Sha'bi who said: The *Sunnah* has not been established through (*sic.* the use of, or resort to) analogies.

حدثنا محمد بن سعيد بن نبات أخبرنا إسماعيل بن إسحاق البصري أخبرنا أحمد بن سعيد بن حزم أخبرنا محمد بن إبراهيم بن حيون الحجازي أخبرنا عبد الله بن أحمد بن حنبل قال سمعت أبي يقول الحديث الضعيف أحب إلينا من الرأي

Muḥammad ibn Sa'eed ibn Nabāt narrated to us Ismā'il ibn Isḥāq al-Baṣri reported to us Aḥmad ibn Sa'eed ibn Ḥazm reported to us Muḥammad ibn Ibrāhim ibn Ḥaywan al-Ḥijāzi reported to us Abdullah ibn Aḥmad ibn Ḥanbal reported to us he said: I heard my father saying: the *Ḍaef* (weak) *ḥadith* is more beloved to me than *Ra'i* (opinion).

حدثنا حمام بن أحمد أخبرنا عباس بن أصبغ حدثنا محمد بن عبد الملك بن أيمن حدثنا عبد الله بن أحمد بن حنبل قال: سألت أبي عن الرجل يكون ببلد لا يجد فيه إلا صاحب حديث لا يعرف صحيحه من سقيمه وأصحاب رأي، فتنزل به النازلة من يسأل؟ فقال أبي يسأل صاحب الحديث ولا يسأل صاحب الرأي، ضعيف الحديث أقوى من رأي أبي حنيفة

Ḥammām ibn Aḥmad narrated to us 'Abbās ibn Aṣbagh reported to us Muḥammad ibn Abdal-Malik ibn 'Ayman narrated to us Abdullah ibn Aḥmad ibn Ḥanbal narrated to us he said: I asked my father about the man in a city in which there is only a man of *ḥadith*; he is only a collector and doesn't know the weak from the strong and a man of *Ra'i.* Then a major problem arises – to whom should he ask? My father said: 'He should ask the man of *ḥadith* and not the man of *Ra'i. Ḍaef* (weak) *ḥadith* is stronger than the *Ra'i* (opinion) of Abu Ḥanifah.'

14. No ruling applies for mistakes or forgetfulness

The law does not apply in relation to forgetfulness and unintentional mistakes as it is established in the Qur'ān and *Sunnah* - except where an exclusion exists or has been made by those texts.[100] Allah the Exalted declares:

وَلَيْسَ عَلَيْكُمْ جُنَاحٌ فِيمَا أَخْطَأْتُم بِهِ وَلَٰكِن مَّا تَعَمَّدَتْ قُلُوبُكُمْ

You will not be blamed if you make a mistake, only for what your hearts deliberately intend.[101]

And He the Exalted and Majestic has also said:

رَبَّنَا لَا تُؤَاخِذْنَا إِن نَّسِينَا أَوْ أَخْطَأْنَا

Our Lord do not take us to task if we forget or make a mistake.[102]

---

[100] No. 105, *al-Muḥalla*, Vol. 1, p. 87
[101] *Qur'ān*, 33: 5
[102] *Qur'ān*, 2: 286

15. Every obligation Allah has obliged all of mankind to do

Concerning every obligation, Allah has obliged all of mankind to adhere to them. If one can do an obligation, it is obligatory to do all of it.[103] If one is unable to do any of it then no obligation applies. And if one is able to do some and leave some, one should do what one can within one's capability, independent of whether this is considered a large or small portion of that obligation. The proof for this is where Allah has said:

لَا يُكَلِّفُ اللَّهُ نَفْسًا إِلَّا وُسْعَهَا

Allah does not burden any soul with more than it can bear.[104]

Moreover, the Prophet peace be upon him has said: '*If I order you to do something, then from it do as much as you can.*'[105] The

[103] No. 106, *al-Muḥalla*, Vol. 1, p. 87

[104] *Qur'ān*, 2: 289

[105] Amongst others, this is found in *Ṣaḥīḥ* Bukhāri: Ismā'il narrated to us Mālik narrated to me from Abu Zinād from al-'Araj from Abu Hurayrah that the Prophet (peace be upon him) said: '*Leave me as I leave you for the people who were before you were ruined because of their questions and their differences over their Prophets. So, if I forbid you to do something, then keep away from it. And if I order you to do something, then do of it as much as you can.*'

isnād of this *ḥadith* has been cited earlier; and with Allah is all success.

16. It is not permissible to perform acts outside of the delineated time parameters

It is not permissible for anyone to do any action in *Deen* which has been timed for a start time or an end time or both, except if the starting time starts or before the end time finishes.[106] In other words, an act which is dependent upon time can only be valid within its specified time (parameters). If it is done *before* its prescribed time it is invalid and if it is done *after* its end-time then it is also invalid. The evidence for that is where Allah has said:

تِلْكَ حُدُودُ اللهِ فَلَا تَعْتَدُوهَا

These are the bounds set by Allah - do not overstep them.[107]

And the Exalted has also said:

وَتِلْكَ حُدُودُ اللهِ وَمَن يَتَعَدَّ حُدُودَ اللهِ فَقَدْ ظَلَمَ نَفْسَهُ

[106] No. 107, *al-Muḥalla*, Vol. 1, pp. 87/88
[107] *Qur'ān*, 2: 229

These are the limits set by Allah - whoever oversteps Allah's limits wrongs his own soul.[108]

The times are limits or demarcation lines which Allah has prescribed - these cannot be flouted without specific (textual) evidence from the Qur'ān or *Sunnah*.

حدثنا عبد الله بن يوسف حدثنا أحمد بن فتح حدثنا عبد الوهاب بن عيسى حدثنا أحمد بن محمد أخبرنا أحمد بن علي أخبرنا مسلم بن الحجاج أخبرنا إسحاق بن إبراهيم هو ابن راهويه عن أبي عامر العقدي حدثنا عبد الله بن جعفر الزهري عن سعد بن إبراهيم بن عبد الرحمن قال: سألت القاسم بن محمد بن أبي بكر الصديق فقال أخبرتني عائشة أن رسول الله صلى الله عليه وسلم قال من عمل عملا ليس عليه أمرنا فهو رد

Abdullah ibn Yusuf narrated to us Aḥmad ibn Fatḥ narrated to us Abd-al Wahāb ibn Esa narrated to us Aḥmad bin Muḥammad narrated to us Aḥmad ibn Ali reported to us Muslim ibn al-Ḥajjāj reported to us Isḥāq – he is ibn Rāhawayh – reported to us from Abu 'Aāmir al-'Aqadi, Abdullah ibn Ja'far al-Zuhri narrated to us from Sa'eed ibn Ibrāhim ibn Abdar-Raḥman, he said - I asked Qāsim ibn Muḥammad al-Ṣadeeq and he said: Aisha informed me that the Messenger of Allah peace and blessings be upon him said: *He who did any act for which there is no sanction from us, it is to be rejected.*[109]

Ali (Ibn Ḥazm) says: when Allah commands someone to do an action that is set within parameters of time that He has

---

[108] *Qur'ān*, 65: 1
[109] The tradition is from *Ṣaḥīḥ* Muslim, but also to be found in most collections of a*ḥādith*.

mentioned, then whoever does the act before or after that specified time, then it is not according to the command of Allah which He has ordained. Hence it is invalid and void and it must be rejected, as it is not the command that Allah has prescribed. But if there is a text which states that it is permissible to do it in another time, then this in reality is a substitute time – therefore Allah has set an original and substitute time, according to the conditions set out in the texts (i.e. Qur'ān and *Sunnah*).

17. The jurist has a higher standing before Allah than the follower

The *Mujtahid*[110] has a higher standing before Allah than the *Muqallid.*[111] This is because even if the *mujtahid* makes a mistake he is still rewarded for undertaking this effort, whereas the person who makes *taqleed* has in fact disobeyed Allah.[112] The point is specified for the people of Islam and doesn't apply to the disbelievers until they embrace Islam. The evidence for this is as follows: the Prophet (peace be upon him) said: '*If he gave a judgment after having tried his best but erred, there is one reward for him.*'[113] We have established earlier that Allah has rebuked *taqleed* – following without evidence. So even if the *Muqallid* obtains the right answer, he is still blameworthy since

[110] The one capable of undertaking *ijtihād*

[111] No. 108, *al-Muḥalla*, Vol. 1, p. 88

[112] For the definition of *taqleed*, see footnote 21.

[113] Only a portion of the *ḥadith* is cited, the full text is: '*When a ḥākim gives a decision, having tried his best to decide correctly and is right, there are two rewards for him; and, if he gave a judgment after having tried his best (to arrive at a correct decision) but erred, there is one reward for him.*' The narration is found in many books, for example: Muslim book 18, no. 4261; Bukhāri book 92, no. 450 and *Sunan* Abu Dāwud book 24, no. 3567

he hasn't approached the matter correctly and has disobeyed Allah whereas the *mujtahid* hasn't.

Whoever follows the Messenger of Allah he is not performing *taqleed.* Rather, it is 'following' because we are commanded to follow him once the evidence is established of his Prophethood. Whoever follows anyone else other than the Messenger of Allah, peace and blessings be upon him, then he has not complied with what Allah has ordered. Regarding the non-Muslims, Allah has stated:

وَمَن يَبْتَغِ غَيْرَ الإِسْلاَمِ دِينًا فَلَن يُقْبَلَ مِنْهُ وَهُوَ فِي الآخِرَةِ مِنَ الْخَاسِرِينَ

If anyone seeks a Deen other than Islam, it will not be accepted from him, he will be one of the losers in the hereafter.[114]

[114] *Qur'ān*, 3: 85

18. Determining the one true viewpoint from among an array

From among all viewpoints (or opinions), there is one that is true, the others besides this are mistaken, and with Allah the Exalted is all *tawfeeq*.[115] Allah the Majestic has said:

فَمَاذَا بَعْدَ الْحَقِّ إِلَّا الضَّلَالُ

Apart from the truth, what is there except error? [116]

وَلَوْ كَانَ مِنْ عِندِ غَيْرِ اللَّهِ لَوَجَدُوا فِيهِ اخْتِلَافًا كَثِيرًا

If it had been from anyone other than Allah, they would have found much inconsistency in it.[117]

And Allah has condemned the matter of *ikhtilāf* (disagreement), He has said:

وَلَا تَكُونُوا كَالَّذِينَ تَفَرَّقُوا وَاخْتَلَفُوا مِن بَعْدِ مَا جَاءَهُمُ الْبَيِّنَاتُ

[115] No. 109, *al-Muḥalla*, Vol. 1, pp. 88/89
[116] *Qur'ān*, 10: 32
[117] *Qur'ān*, 4: 82

Do not be like those who, after they have been given clear revelation, split into factions and fall into disputes.[118]

وَلَا تَنَازَعُوا فَتَفْشَلُوا وَتَذْهَبَ رِيحُكُمْ وَاصْبِرُوا إِنَّ اللَّهَ مَعَ الصَّابِرِينَ

And do not quarrel with one another, or you may lose heart and your spirit may desert you. Be steadfast: Allah is with the steadfast.[119]

وَنَزَّلْنَا عَلَيْكَ الْكِتَابَ تِبْيَانًا لِّكُلِّ شَيْءٍ

For We have sent the Scripture down to you explaining everything.[120]

Thus, it is well established that the truth in all viewpoints must be what Allah has judged, (what is) determined to be as such, and it is one (truth) with no disagreement. Whatever is false is definitely not from Allah. Whoever has claimed that all statements resulting from *ijtihād* are all correct, and that every *mujtahid* is correct, then he has expressed a statement which is not established in the Qur'ān, *Sunnah*, *Ijmā'*, or even from reason; whatever is like that must definitely be void. What also erases that (viewpoint) is what the Messenger of Allah peace be upon him said: '*If a Ḥākim performs ijtihād and errors, he has a single reward.*'[121] So the text (from him) peace and blessings be upon him, establishes that a *mujtahid* can be mistaken. Whoever has said the people are ordered to follow their *ijtihād*, this is mistaken, because the order is to only follow what Allah has

---

[118] *Qur'ān*, 3: 105
[119] *Qur'ān*, 8: 46
[120] *Qur'ān*, 16: 89
[121] See footnote 113 and 124.

revealed and try to achieve (or determine) what Allah the exalted has ordered of them.[122] Allah the Exalted has said:

اتَّبِعُوا مَا أُنزِلَ إِلَيْكُم مِّن رَّبِّكُمْ وَلَا تَتَّبِعُوا مِن دُونِهِ أَوْلِيَاءَ

Follow what has been sent down to you from your Lord; do not follow other masters beside Him.[123]

The Almighty has ordered us to follow what has been revealed to us and not to follow others and not to exceed his limits. Rather, the reward of the *mujtahid* when mistaken is one reward for his intention is to seek the truth only, and he is not sinful because Allah has forgiven that. But if he manages to reach (or achieve) the truth he gets another reward, because the Prophet peace and blessings be upon him said, '*...he will obtain a second reward.*'

حدثنا عبد الرحمن بن عبد الله بن خالد أخبرنا إبراهيم بن أحمد الفربري حدثنا البخاري حدثنا عبد الله بن يزيد المقري حدثنا حيوة بن شريح حدثنا يزيد بن عبد الله بن الهاد عن محمد بن إبراهيم بن الحارث عن بسر بن سعيد عن أبي قيس مولى عمرو بن العاص عن عمرو بن العاص أنه سمع رسول الله صلى الله عليه وسلم يقول إذا حكم الحاكم فاجتهد ثم أصاب فله أجران، وإذا حكم فاجتهد ثم أخطأ فله أجر

Abdar-Raḥman ibn Abdullah ibn Khālid narrated to us Ibrāhim ibn Aḥmad al-Firabry reported to us al-Bukhāri narrated to us Abdullah ibn Yazeed al-Muqri narrated to

---

[122] A very subtle point is being made here. Ibn Ḥazm is arguing that the order is not to do *ijtihād* per se, but to follow what Allah has revealed and determine what he has ordered. Thus, in a given situation, it is necessary to perform *ijtihād* in order to reach what has been ordered. During that process, if the *mujtahid* makes a mistake he is forgiven for that shortcoming. If the truth is reached, then a double-reward is received.

[123] *Qur'ān*, 7: 3

> us Ḥaywa ibn Shurayḥ narrated to us Yazeed ibn Abdullah ibn al-Ahād narrated to us from Muḥammad ibn Ibrāhim ibn al-Ḥārith from Busr ibn Sa'eed from Abu Qays, *mawla* of 'Amr ibn al-'Aāṣ from 'Amr ibn al-'Aāṣ that he heard the Messenger of Allah peace and blessings be upon him saying: *If a Ḥākim gives a verdict according to his ijtihād and is correct he will receive a double reward, and if a Ḥākim performs ijtihād and errors, he has a single reward.*[124]

It isn't permissible to rule at all originally by guesswork, as Allah the Exalted has said:

وَمَا لَهُم بِهِ مِنْ عِلْمٍ إِن يَتَّبِعُونَ إِلَّا الظَّنَّ وَإِنَّ الظَّنَّ لَا يُغْنِي مِنَ الْحَقِّ شَيْئًا

They have no knowledge to base this on: they merely follow guesswork. Guesswork is of no value against the truth.[125]

And the Messenger of Allah peace and blessings be upon him has said: '*Beware of guesswork, for guesswork is the worst of false tales.*'[126]
And with Allah the Almighty is all *tawfeeq*.

---

[124] Recorded by al-Bukhāri in the book of holding fast to the Qur'ān and *Sunnah*. The same narration is also cited widely, appearing in the collections of Muslim, Abu Dāwud and many others.
[125] *Qur'ān*, 53: 28
[126] Agreed upon. This authentic narration appears across the entire corpus of *ḥadith*. The *matn* (reported wording) and *isnād* of al-Bukhāri is: Abdullah ibn Yusuf narrated to us Mālik reported to us from Abi Zinād from al-'Araj from Abu Hurayrah (may Allah be pleased with him) said that the Messenger of Allah peace and blessings be upon him said: '*Beware of guesswork, for guesswork is the worst of false tales. And do not look for others faults, and do not do spying on one another, and do not outbid one another (with a view to raising the price), and do not be jealous of one another and do not hate one another, and do not desert (stop talking to) one another. And O, Allah's worshipers! Be brothers!*'

Made in the USA
Las Vegas, NV
01 April 2025

20421177R00046